AEI Legislative Analyses
Balanced analyses of current proposals before the Congress, prepared with the help of specialists in law, economics, and government

Regulatory Reform for Motor Carriers

An Analysis of Pending Legislation

1980
96th Congress
2nd Session

American Enterprise Institute
for Public Policy Research
Washington, D.C.

ISBN 0-8447-0230-7
Legislative Analysis No. 15, 96th Congress
April 1980

Contents

1

Introduction

Since 1935 Congress has given the Interstate Commerce Commission (ICC) power to regulate a great many aspects of the motor carrier industry. The ICC regulates entry into the trucking business, the routes that each firm can use and the commodities each firm can carry, the rates charged by truckers, and the operations of classes of carriers otherwise exempt from regulation. In 1948, over the veto of President Truman, collective rate setting by carriers' rate bureaus was exempted from the antitrust laws. Thus regulated carriers compete for the most part on the basis of quality of service, as the airlines did before the 1978 legislation that gradually deregulates that industry.

Since 1948 every administration has sought in varying degrees to reduce the scope of this regulatory authority, with limited success. (See the following chapter.) Nevertheless, recent economic and political pressures for change in the entire federal regulatory system and the specific demand for regulatory restructuring in the motor carrier field have intensified the debate among the proponents and opponents of change. The determination of a majority of the commission to proceed with deregulation if Congress does not act shortly has increased the likelihood that Congress will enact comprehensive reform legislation in this legislative session.

This legislative analysis will examine the principal reform proposals and the major arguments for and against the most significant changes that are proposed as they affect economic regulation. This analysis will deal with carriers of property rather than carriers of passengers and with regulation of interstate carriers as distinguished from intrastate carriers.

2

Background

Regulated motor carriers of property may include 17,000 trucking companies. The largest 100 companies generate more than half of the total revenues of the largest 4,000 companies. About 1,050 trucking companies have annual revenues exceeding $3 million a year and 2,900 trucking companies have revenues between $500,000 and $3 million a year. Many trucking activities are not subject to economic regulation. The largest number of truckers that escape regulation are those that haul exempt property, such as raw agricultural products. Firms that are not primarily in the trucking business are permitted to act as private carriers hauling their own products in trucks that they own or operate. There has been much growth in the trucking activities of these so-called private carriers in recent years.[1]

Congress has acted to gradually deregulate the airlines, and legislation is pending to reduce government regulation of rail carriers. However, the trucking industry generates roughly $108 billion in revenues annually, or about 75 percent of the revenues earned by all forms of transportation. Thus the trucking industry is much larger than the airline industry, which is being deregulated under 1978 legislation.[2] Clearly the issue of whether to reform the regulation of regulated motor carriers of property and the directions and specifics of reform are of great importance to the carriers involved, the shippers, and consumers generally.

The shock of the Penn Central Railroad bankruptcy stimulated recent attempts to reform economic regulation of transportation at the federal level. The Nixon administration's Transportation Regulatory Modernization Act, submitted in 1971, would have dealt with regulatory reform for rail, truck, and water carriers in one bill. Under that bill, carriers could have adjusted fares up or down within a certain range, called a zone of rate freedom. Ceilings on rates would have been keyed in part to the competition or lack of competition that a carrier or carriers in a particular mode of transportation, such as trucking, had from carriers in another mode of transportation, such as rail. The bill would have cut back antitrust immunity for collective rate making by motor carriers and would have made it easier for new motor carriers to enter the regulated transportation marketplace. Provision would have been made to ease route and other restrictions that cause inefficient trucking operations.[3]

The Ford administration chose to deal with reducing the regulation of the various transportation modes in separate legislation. President Ford's message to Congress of November 13, 1975, endorsed the proposed Motor Carrier Reform Act of 1975. This legislation would have provided a gradually expanding zone of rate freedom. The bill would have made it more difficult for a carrier to obtain ICC suspension of the effectiveness of competing rate offerings. This provision was designed to encourage innovative rates adapted to shippers' needs.

The Ford proposal went well beyond the Transportation Regulatory Modernization Act of 1971 in its proposed reduction of antitrust immunity for carriers' collective rate making and related activities. The 1975 bill would have required the ICC to act on rate offerings within certain time limits and would have prevented competing carriers from claiming discrimination against shippers. The bill would also have made it easier to enter the regulated market, would have allowed exempt carriers to haul regulated commodities on return trips (backhauls) under certain conditions, and would have reduced restrictions imposing inefficiencies on truckers.[4]

Neither of these proposals won congressional approval, but features of each may be found in proposals currently being considered by the Congress.

On June 21, 1979, President Carter transmitted to Congress his administration's proposal for reducing motor carrier regulation. He stated:

> This system of detailed regulation was imposed in 1935 when the trucking industry was in its infancy, and when the Nation was in the midst of its most serious depression. At that time, competition was blamed for the Nation's economic woes. Many believed that extensive government control was needed to protect the newly developing trucking industry.
>
> In the 44 years since regulation was first imposed, conditions have changed dramatically. The trucking industry has matured and prospered, and our economy has become strong. But our system of regulation has remained basically the same. . . .
>
> Our current regulatory system contributes to three of our Nation's most pressing problems—inflation, excessive government regulation and the shortage of energy. Since regulation permits price-fixing and stifles price competition, consumers are unnecessarily paying billions of dollars a year in higher transportation prices. During these inflationary times, government policies that needlessly raise costs cannot be tolerated. . . .
>
> Finally, regulation needlessly wastes our Nation's precious fuel by preventing carriers from making the most productive use of their equipment, and by requiring empty backhauls and circuitous routings.
>
> The legislation I am proposing will restore the competitive spirit to the trucking industry, reduce inflation, minimize government regulation and save energy.

Senator Edward M. Kennedy (D-Mass.), who joined with the administration in shaping the legislation, announced that it would reduce substantially ICC regulation of the trucking industry and eliminate the industry's current antitrust immunity.[5] This legislation was introduced as S. 1400 by Senator Kennedy and five cosponsors and as H.R. 4586 by Representatives Harold T. Johnson (D-Calif.) and Peter W. Rodino, Jr. (D-N.J.).

The Carter–Kennedy legislation was strongly opposed by the National Brotherhood of Teamsters and the American Trucking Associations, Inc. (ATA), and was supported by a number of associations of large and small shippers, farmer cooperatives, and consumer organizations.

House and Senate committees held hearings on this and other alternative proposals. The debate in those hearings concentrated primarily on five central issues. These issues involved:

- Easing restrictions on new entry
- Eliminating existing limitations on commodities, circuitous routing, and gateway restrictions and other restraints that are alleged to cause empty backhauls and similar inefficiencies
- Expansion of agricultural trucking exemptions
- Increased freedom of carrier rate making without ICC interference
- Eliminating or further circumscribing the antitrust immunity for rate bureaus.

After extensive hearings had been held, Senator Howard W. Cannon (D-Nev.), chairman of the Senate Committee on Commerce, Science and Transportation, and Senator Bob Packwood (R-Oreg.), ranking minority member of that committee, introduced S. 2245. This bill amounted to a compromise proposal for regulatory reform. In his statement on introducing the bill, Senator Cannon noted, "I have given my personal commitment to doing everything in my power to see that a bill is on the desk of the President by no later than June 1, 1980."[6] On March 24, 1980, the Senate Committee on Commerce, Science and Transportation favorably reported an amended version of S. 2245. The Senate passed S. 2245 with amendments on April 15, 1980.[7]

In addition to the Senate legislation, initial hearings have been held on reform legislation in the House although no action has been taken by the House committee pending Senate action.

Although various House and Senate versions dealing with regulation of trucking differ in significant respects, the central issues remain the same. The focus continues on the relative economic and social gains and losses inherent in the status quo versus a changed regulatory environment. The following analysis reviews key features and differences in the pending Senate and House legislation and explores the arguments surrounding the issues raised by the legislation.

In dealing with all these issues, one overall problem confronted by the Congress is that of the degree of specificity that should be included in legislation. If too many details and regulatory requirements are spelled out, regulatory authorities may lack the flexibility needed to meet the changing environment that partial deregulation will bring. If Congress is not specific enough, the regulatory agency may undertake initiatives that Congress never intended. Congress has the dilemma of deciding whether to give only policy guidance in general terms or to spell out the limits of the regulatory agency's discretion.

3

Principal Features of Senate and House Legislation

Motor Carrier Reform Act of 1980 (S. 2245)

S. 2245, which the Senate passed on April 15, 1980, would instruct the Interstate Commerce Commission to follow a new national transportation policy, favoring competition and greater efficiency in motor carrier regulation. For many years the existing national transportation policy, set forth as a preamble to the Interstate Commerce Act, has been interpreted by the commission as a mandate to protect existing carriers from the challenge of new entrants so that those carriers already in the system could enjoy a stable financial return. S. 2245 would instruct the commission to encourage price and service alternatives; to achieve energy and economic efficiency; to provide "opportunities for adequate profits and fair wages"; to provide and maintain service to small communities and small shippers; to provide a "sound, safe, and competitive motor carrier system"; to promote carrier participation by minorities; and to promote intermodal transportation. The chairman of the Senate Committee on Commerce, Science and Transportation notes that this bill does not deregulate the motor carrier industry but that it does ensure increased competition. The report of the committee states, "It is clearly the committee's intent that national transportation policy must recognize the importance of competition as the most desirable means for achieving transportation goals."[8]

It is unclear, however, how the ICC will follow the policy of greater competition, as other concerns outlined in the policy statement may at times conflict with the goal of encouraging competition. For example, many would perceive the injunction to provide "opportunities for adequate profits and fair wages" as an instruction to limit competition to at least some degree. A monopolist is more likely to enjoy "adequate profits," while firms in a highly competitive industry may at times have slimmer profit margins.

Nevertheless, it seems clear that the Senate seeks to install a new cornerstone of national transportation policy—the encouragement of competition and efficiency through regulatory decision making—and to eliminate the artificial barriers that the ICC has in the past established to protect motor carriers already in the market. The Senate also intends to see that the policy is implemented by requiring oversight hearings at least each year during the first five years after enactment of S. 2245.

Liberalized Entry Policy. Section 5 of S. 2245 establishes a new entry test to be used by the ICC in reviewing applications by carriers seeking to enter a market or by existing carriers seeking to expand their operating sphere.

ICC standards applied at present require a would-be entrant to show (1) that it is fit, willing, and able to provide the proposed service, and (2) that the entry is required by existing or future public convenience and necessity. At present the applicant bears the burden of proof as to both tests. Carriers already in the market can defeat the application by showing that there is adequate service already in place and that the new entrant would take traffic away from those already in the market.

Under S. 2245, a part of the burden of proof would be shifted from the applicant to competing carriers already in the market. The ICC would have to grant a certificate allowing the new carrier to serve the market *unless* it finds by a preponderance of the evidence that the proposed service would be inconsistent with present or future public convenience or necessity. This standard would create the presumption that the proposed service meets the public convenience and necessity and is in the public interest.

The commission is specifically instructed to consider the new national transportation policy supporting competition and to consider evidence of public support for the application. The ICC may also consider the effect that granting the application would have upon existing carriers, but it may not use projected diversion of revenues or traffic from existing carriers to a new carrier as the sole basis for denying entry of the new carrier. The Senate committee eliminated language in S. 2245 that would have allowed the commission to deny a certificate on its own initiative. According to the report of the committee, "this means that there must be sufficient evidence on the record introduced by the parties to the proceeding to justify denial of the application."[9]

The parties to the proceeding must also be "interested" parties. The bill limits opposing carriers to (1) those that have provided service within the scope of the application within the preceding twelve months and are willing and able to provide service that meets the reasonable needs of the shippers involved, and (2) competing new applicants. The commission can also grant leave to intervene to other carriers if they show legitimate interests not contrary to the new national transportation policy.

The bill would also eliminate the public convenience and necessity test in specific cases. The test would not apply to (1) applications for authority to serve any community not already served by any motor carrier certificated by the ICC; (2) transportation services substituted for abandoned rail service to a community; (3) certain services in which the federal government is a shipper; and (4) package shipments involving less than 100 pounds per package. With respect to these services the applicant need only show that it is fit, willing, and able to provide the service. Each petition for entry must be adjudicated individually; proposals to grant "master certificates" for new entry were rejected.

Removal of Restrictions on Operating Authority. The Senate bill instructs the ICC to eliminate artificial restrictions on operating authority now in effect. At present the commission grants operating certificates that limit the territorial scope of a motor carrier's activity, the route the carrier must follow, the commodities it can handle, and the interim points along the route at which the carrier may stop and make pickups and deliveries. This regulatory regime, critics charge, creates industry inefficiency and waste in the form of empty backhauls, circuitous routings, and other limitations.

The bill requires that the commission, within six months of enactment of the legislation, eliminate gateway and circuitous route restrictions from motor carrier certificates. (A gateway is the geographical point at which a carrier combines or "tacks" together two separate routes authorized by the ICC. Traffic moving from one route to the other must pass through the gateway.) It also requires that within the same period the commission develop procedures to permit the removal of additional unreasonable operating restrictions that are inefficient, waste energy, or are contrary to the public interest. The ICC is instructed to "reasonably" broaden commodity authorizations, eliminate interim point restrictions, provide round-trip authority to deal with empty backhauls, and to broaden excessively narrow territorial limitations. The commission is instructed to consider the impact of removal of restrictions on energy conservation, efficiency, and the national transportation policy. It is also required to give special consideration to providing and maintaining service to small communities and small shippers.

Additional Exemptions from Regulation. Under existing law, certain types of transportation services are exempted from ICC regulation. Generally this is in the agricultural area, and involves fresh fruits and vegetables and unprocessed poultry, fish, and livestock. S. 2245 would extend the exemption to include all livestock; all food products for human consumption, whether processed or not; seeds; animal feed; plants; agricultural limestone and other soil conditioners; and nonhazardous agricultural chemicals and fertilizers. Mixed loads of regulated and unregulated commodities could also be carried in the same vehicle.

The bill would also ease restrictions on backhauls. An owner-operator exempt from economic regulation could haul regulated commodities in competition with regulated carriers on the return trip after delivering exempt commodities on the prime haul. On such backhaul trips, the trucker must charge a rate equal to or exceeding the lowest rate in effect for a certificated common carrier, and must meet registration requirements.

Carriers that move goods primarily by air and use trucks only incidentally to pick up and deliver would be exempt from ICC regulation. In addition,

S. 2245 removes ICC powers over the transportation of pallets and other shipping devices, as well as used empty shipping containers, such as intermodal containers used in both water and land transportation.

Limits on Application of the Robinson-Patman Act. The Federal Trade Commission has ruled that the anti-price discrimination provisions of the Robinson-Patman Antidiscrimination Act of 1914 prevent a seller of food and grocery products that charges a uniform delivered price from giving a discount to a customer who picks up the product at the seller's plant with his own trucks. The pending legislation would allow for such a discount. The discount must reflect the actual cost of transportation that the seller would otherwise bear. If the seller gives such a discount to one customer who makes his own pickup, the discount must be given to all such purchases on a nondiscriminatory basis.

Broader Definition of Exempt Private Carriage. Section 9 of the bill allows members of a corporate family in which the parent corporation has a 100 percent interest to provide transportation for other members of the corporate family without ICC regulation. The parent company must notify the commission of its intent to provide such transportation, listing the participating subsidiaries; the ICC must publish a notice in the *Federal Register;* and each vehicle operated by the company actually providing the transportation must carry a copy of the notice.

Eliminating the "Rule of Eight" for Contract Carriers. In the past, the ICC limited the definition of a contract carrier to a carrier that serves no more than eight shippers. The commission recently abandoned the so-called rule of eight. S. 2245 ratifies that action and eliminates restrictions on the number of shippers that may be served by a contract carrier. It also permits a single carrier to serve as both a contract and common carrier. A permit must be granted to a contract carrier unless approval would endanger an existing common carrier to "an extent contrary to the public interest."

Restricting Antitrust Immunity for Rate Bureau Activities. Regulated motor carriers have enjoyed limited immunity from the antitrust laws since the enactment of the Reed-Bulwinkle Act in 1948, over President Truman's veto. That legislation permits collective action by carriers (through rate bureaus) to propose rates for ICC approval.

This immunity from the antitrust laws is significantly cut back by S.2245. Starting July 1, 1983, no rate bureau agreement may be approved by the ICC to discuss or vote upon single-line rates. A single-line rate is a rate charge or allowance by a single motor carrier that applies only over its line for goods that can be carried from the shipper to the customer on that carrier alone, without transferring to another carrier. Joint-line through rates between two or more carriers are not affected by this amendment.

In addition to this withdrawal of antitrust immunity, the bill also restricts certain activities of the rate bureaus:

- A rate bureau may not interfere with any carrier's right of independent rate action and may not file a protest with the ICC if an individual carrier files an independent rate.
- After January 1, 1981, voting on specific rates may only occur among carriers that actually have the authority to participate in the transportation to which the discussion applies.
- A bureau must tell anyone who asks the name of the firm that proposed a rule or rate docketed with it. A bureau must open its rate-making and rule-making meetings to anyone who wants to attend. The bureau must also divulge to any person the vote cast by any member carrier on any proposal before the bureau.

The bureau must act within 120 days of the time a rule or rate is docketed with it, unless an extension of time, subject to review by the commission, is required by unusual circumstances.

Rate bureaus could continue to handle general rate increases for single-line and other rates after 1983 notwithstanding the prohibition against single-line rate discussions or voting. The committee report specifies, however, that any general rate increase discussions by the carriers must be limited to industry average costs and may not include discussion of specific markets or individual single-line rates.

The bill would set up a study commission to recommend ways to deal with antitrust immunity. The study group's report would be due one year before the prohibition against single-line collective rate making takes effect. Conceivably the study commission's recommendation could result in an amendment either eliminating or broadening the antitrust immunity provided in S. 2245. The study commission would be composed of industry representatives and members of the House and Senate, assisted by liaison officers of the various affected federal agencies, including the Department of Transportation, the ICC, the Federal Trade Commission, and the Department of Justice.

A Zone of Rate Freedom. S. 2245 would establish a zone of rate freedom within which rates would be free from suspension or revocation by ICC on the ground that they were unreasonably high or unreasonably low. Carriers could lower or raise rates by as much as 10 percent of the rate that was in effect one year before the new rate takes effect. If carriers want to promulgate even lower rates, the new rates can be as much as 10 percent below the rate in effect July 1, 1980. The ICC would be authorized to increase the zone of rate freedom by up to 5 percent a year if it finds that actual or potential competition is strong enough to keep rates within bounds and that carriers, shippers, and the public would benefit from increased rate flexibility.

On July 1, 1983, truckers and truckers' organizations that discuss and vote on single-line rates will no longer be immune from antitrust laws. After that date, the base rate will be the rate in effect one year prior to the effective date of the new rate, adjusted to reflect changes in the producers' price index, thus allowing truckers to recoup extra costs caused by inflation. Before that date adjustments would be made to include the amount of general rate increases approved by the ICC except for the first 5 percent of such increases in the year.

Any rate implemented by a carrier under the zone of rate freedom provision would remain subject to the antitrust laws. The ICC could suspend and investigate discriminatory rates and those that constitute predatory practices contrary to national transportation policy. According to the committee report, the ICC would have primary jurisdiction to enforce the antitrust laws but "to the extent that there are judicial actions that the commission is not authorized to bring on its own behalf, there will then be the need for the Justice Department to intervene in order to bring a court action."

Rule of Rate Making—Inflationary Relief. Rate increases under the bill would be allowed to enable motor carriers to recoup inflationary costs anticipated in the future. Under existing legislation general rate increases are granted to motor carriers based on increased costs they have already experienced. The bill will provide for "prospective relief," requiring the ICC to allow a rate base that takes into account future anticipated escalating costs. This provision is designed to allow rate structures to anticipate even further inflationary increases in costs to the carrier.

Miscellaneous Provisions. S. 2245 also would make it unlawful to coerce or attempt to coerce motor vehicle operators or owners to employ loading or unloading assistance from so-called lumpers that consignors or consignees do not require or that the owner or operator of the motor vehicle would not otherwise provide. The bill further provides for a fit-willing-and-able test for motor carrier brokers on regulated commodities; a requirement for written contracts on exempt agricultural movements; an increase from 15 percent to 35 percent in the total tonnage that agricultural co-ops may haul in nonmember nonagricultural freight (allowing for greater use of co-op trucks); commission authority to require reasonable joint rates and through routes from one motor carrier to another and with rail express and water common carriers when such action is shown to be necessary; liberalized commission authority to provide for emergency temporary authority on an expedited basis; and additional procedural changes. The ICC would be required to study motor carrier service to communities of 5,000 and under and report to the president and Congress by September 1, 1981.

Principal Differences between S. 2245 and the Carter–Kennedy Bill

S. 1400, entitled the Trucking Competition and Safety Act of 1979, was introduced by Senator Edward M. Kennedy and five cosponsors and reflects the agreement of the administration on trucking regulatory reform. H.R. 4586, introduced in the House of Representatives by Representatives Harold T. Johnson and Peter W. Rodino, Jr., is identical. Because the administration has subsequently indicated its acceptance of S. 2245, only the principal differences between the two bills will be outlined here.

The national transportation policy statement in the Carter–Kennedy bill would go further than S. 2245 as passed by the Senate. (All comparisons in this section are with S. 2245 as passed by the Senate.) The Carter–Kennedy bill calls for maximum reliance on competitive market forces to provide transportation services at competitive prices. Regulatory barriers to entry would be lowered as a way to reduce the concentration of market power in certain carriers.

The Carter–Kennedy bill adds criteria to be considered in determining public convenience and necessity not found in S. 2245. These include lowering an applicant's operating costs, reducing transit time and avoiding interchanges, meeting user and consumer preferences for service, producing lower rates, improving the competitive climate in an area, and so forth. Contract motor carriers would not have standing to contest entry.

Restrictions on intermediate stops or restrictions that require one-way haulage would be removed by the ICC within thirty days of the carrier's petition. ICC rules would make it easier to eliminate gateway and routing restrictions. No new authorization would be restricted to a single shipper or plant, unless requested by the carrier. Commodity restrictions would be phased out over three years. The ICC would have to act within ninety days on applications to remove restrictions that make service circuitous or costly.

Carriage exempt from regulation in the Carter–Kennedy bill would include tractors and machinery used in agricultural production but not used pallets and other shipping devices. After two years, truckload traffic over 10,000 pounds, under a single bill of lading, or transported by carriers other than general freight carriers would be exempt from regulation. (Shipments of more than 10,000 pounds are regarded as truckload shipments and usually carry a lower rate than less-than-truckload shipments.) The Carter–Kennedy bill would authorize the ICC to exempt from all regulation or from particular regulations any person or class of persons if it finds this consistent with national transportation policy. The exemption for private carriage is broader in that corporations and groups of corporations, including unincorporated divisions, could provide compensated motor carriage for members of the corporate family if as much as 50 percent of their voting stock is owned, and the ICC could prescribe a lesser percentage that it determines to be adequate for control.[10] Contract carriers would be authorized to set joint and through rates with common carriers including rail, express, and water carriers.

The zone of rate freedom in the Carter–Kennedy bill would favor the downward movement of rates. In the first two years, rates could be increased 5 percent or reduced 20 percent per year and such changes would be presumed reasonable. After two years, yearly increases could amount to 7 percent within the zone and no downward limit would be imposed so long as the rate equaled or exceeded the carrier's variable cost of providing the transportation to which the rate applied.

The ICC would be given certain additional factors to consider in prescribing rates, classifications, rules, or practices. These factors would include national transportation policy, off-peak pricing, and a carrier's varying prices to meet particular competitive conditions. Other language that S. 2245 includes in the section dealing with rates is not included in the Carter–Kennedy bill, nor does that bill permit consideration of anticipated future costs. However, it would reduce the period of notice required for rate increases and, after five years, rate increases could be effective on publication.

The Carter–Kennedy bill would eliminate antitrust immunity for actions of rate bureaus immediately. This end to immunity would not be limited to single-line rates. The study called for by the bill is not limited to antitrust immunity; the Secretary of Transportation, ICC, and Department of Justice would report January 1, 1983, on the implementation of the statute and whether continued regulation of motor carriers is required. The Secretary of Transportation would report specifically on whether the test of the public convenience and necessity should be continued.

The Carter–Kennedy bill would make it more difficult for the ICC to suspend or delay the effective date of rates. Carriers, however, would have to account for all amounts recovered from increased rates for up to three months and the ICC could order refunds and direct that a carrier pay the attorneys' fees and costs of successful contestants. If a contestant acted in bad faith, the ICC could require it to pay attorneys' fees and costs to the carrier.

The ICC could not approve consolidations, mergers, and acquisitions for five years after enactment of the bill if it found that competition would decrease, that a monopoly would be created, or that trade would be restrained. However, such mergers could be approved if the ICC found that the anticompetitive effects were outweighed by the public interest in meeting significant transportation needs, and that these needs could not be satisfactorily met otherwise. The ICC would not be involved in antitrust enforcement after five years.

Other differences include omission of provisions as to lumpers (laborers employed to load or unload freight) and the Robinson–Patman Act. Cooperatives could carry up to as much tonnage for others as they carried for themselves. Motor carriers would not be required to set joint and through rates.

The Carter–Kennedy bill would preempt conflicting state and local laws and rules. It also contains extensive provisions on motor carrier safety and safety enforcement not found in S. 2245.

The Motor Carrier Act of 1980 (H.R. 6418)

The House Public Works and Transportation Committee is considering a reform bill introduced by four of its members. That bill, H.R. 6418, introduced by Representative James J. Howard (D-N.J.) and three cosponsors, is currently before the Subcommittee on Surface Transportation. Hearings have been held and markup of a deregulation bill is expected shortly, as this is written. Key features of H.R. 6418, along with some comparisons with the Senate bill, are set forth below.

National Transportation Policy. H.R. 6418 would amend the national transportation policy preamble to the Interstate Commerce Act by requiring the ICC to consider promotion of efficient transportation services in order (1) to meet the needs of shippers and receivers; (2) to allow a variety of quality and price options to meet changing market demands; (3) to achieve maximum utilization of equipment and energy resources; (4) to enable efficient and well-managed carriers to earn adequate profits, attract capital, and maintain and promote fair wages and working conditions; (5) to improve service to small communities and on small shipments; and (6) to maintain and promote a safe, sound, and competitive motor carrier system for the transportation of property.

Although a "competitive motor carrier system" is one of the goals to be sought under the bill, unlike the Senate version, it is only one such goal and presumably would not be given overriding importance by the regulators administering the statute.

Liberalized Entry Policy. Section 5 of H.R. 6418 retains the public convenience and necessity test, but instructs the commission to consider the new transportation policy set forth in the legislation, to consider evidence of public support for an entry application, and to consider quality and quantity of available service. However, this section prohibits the commission from finding "that diversion of revenue or traffic from an existing carrier to be in and of itself inconsistent with the public convenience and necessity."

Unlike the Senate version, the burden of proof with respect to a showing of public convenience and necessity remains with the applicant and is not shifted in part to competing carriers already in the market. The House version is also silent as to whether the commission may decline to grant an application on its own motion. The requirement that the ICC adjudicate such applications on the record made before the commission would seem to preclude that.

In other respects, the motor carrier entry provision in H.R. 6418 is virtually identical to the entry provision in the Senate bill. The opposing carriers must have an interest in the particular traffic involved or be competing for the new authority, or intervene pursuant to leave of the commission upon a showing that the carrier has interests that are "not contrary" to the new national transportation policy.

The House bill would also eliminate public convenience and necessity tests in specified areas. Exempted are applications for authority to provide new service to "any point not served by a motor carrier"; substitute transportation for an abandoned railroad service; certain instances in which the federal government is the shipper; and shipments of 100 pounds or less if no item in a truck exceeds that amount.

Reduction of Restrictions on Operating Authority. H.R. 6418 would require the commission to set up a procedure within six months for processing applications of motor carriers seeking removal of operating restrictions to eliminate gateway or circuitous route limitations. It would also require the ICC to broaden the categories of commodities authorized by the carrier certificate; to provide for transportation service to intermediate points on the carrier's route; to provide round-trip authority where only one-way authority exists; to eliminate unreasonable or excessively narrow territorial limitations; or to eliminate any other restriction that is wasteful of fuel or inefficient. H.R. 6418 does not require the commission within the same 180-day period to eliminate gateway restrictions and circuitous route limitations on its own, a feature of the Senate bill. Moreover, H.R. 6418 would place upon the applicant seeking the removal of a restriction the burden of proof that the proposed removal of a restriction will result in fuel savings or improved efficiency. The burden of proof on other issues in any such expedited proceeding would be on the party opposing the application for restriction removal. The Senate bill has no specific provision as to the burden of proof with respect to these provisions.

Further Exemptions from Regulation. H.R. 6418 would extend the agricultural exemption in a much more limited fashion than the Senate bill. It would exempt all livestock feed, poultry feed, and agricultural seeds and plants *if* the commodities are transported to an agricultural production site or a business enterprise selling to agricultural producers of goods used in agricultural production. Unlike the Senate bill, H.R. 6418 would not extend the exemption to food products processed for human consumption, and it would limit the agricultural products that are added to the exemption by requiring that they be shipped directly to the farmer or to a farmer's supplier. Exempt products could be moved in mixed loads with products whose transportation is subject to regulation. A new section would be added, however, allowing owner-operator exemption for backhaul performed completely on behalf of the owner when the immediately preceding haulage was that of exempt property, the return is to the area of origin of the preceding haulage, and the owner-operator complies with certain minimum rate and registration requirements.

With respect to transportation of commodities by truck as a service incidental to air services, again the House version is more narrowly drawn. The bill would exempt truck transportation to a radius of thirty-five miles or less of an airport or designated airport city, whichever is greater, when it is part of a continuous movement under a through air bill of lading. Substituted motor carrier service for air service is also exempted in cases in which the service is provided at the expense of the air carrier or air freight forwarder in emergency situations arising from the inability of the airline to perform air transportation due to adverse weather conditions or equipment failure.

Wider Exemption of Private Carriage. Section 9 of the H.R. 6418 would allow a corporation to carry property for itself or for a subsidiary or an affiliated corporation for compensation free of economic regulation. This exemption is broader than the one in the Senate version in that H.R. 6418 does not require that each subsidiary or affiliate must be 100 percent owned by a common parent. Notice provisions are nearly alike in the two bills.

Broader Authority for Contract Carriers. H.R. 6418 broadens the definition of contract carrier of property. Section 10 amends the Interstate Commerce Act to provide that a contract carrier of property includes a carrier that operates under continuing agreements with one or more persons (with no express limit as to number) which are assigned motor vehicles for a continuing period of time for the exclusive use of such persons or designed to meet the distinct needs of each such person. This presumably is intended to eliminate the "rule of eight" once applied by the commission that limited the number of shippers a contract carrier could serve. A single carrier may also serve as both a common carrier and contract carrier, but H.R. 6418 allows for such dual operation over the same route or in the same area only if the commission finds that holding both a common carrier certificate and a contract permit will result in a more balanced and fuel-efficient operation and will otherwise be in the public interest. The burden in the H.R. 6418 would appear to be placed upon the person seeking the dual authority, whereas the Senate version appears to place the burden on those opposing the dual authority.

Continuation of Rate Bureau Antitrust Immunity. H.R. 6418 does not limit collective rate making among single-line carriers. Thus, it continues antitrust immunity for rate discussions and votes among competing carriers in a particular service even though any of the carriers might provide this service alone.

H.R. 6418 also provides that a rate bureau may docket and handle rates for intrastate transportation with specific authorization from the state involved. The Senate version of the bill originally contained this provision but it was deleted after objections by the Department of Justice. Other reforms affecting rate bureaus contained in the original Senate bill are included in H.R. 6418, such as limiting voting to carriers that may engage in carriage covered by the rate in issue.

A Zone of Rate Flexibility. H.R. 6418 provides that the commission may not suspend or investigate any rate to determine whether or not such rate is unreasonably high or unreasonably low if the rate is not more than 10 percent above or below the rate in effect one year prior to its effective date. In the case of downward rate flexibility, the bill would allow a greater reduction by permitting a 10 percent reduction from the rates in effect on July 1, 1980. The bill reserves the right of the commission to suspend and investigate rates for suspected discriminatory effect or predatory practices.

Rate-making Standards. H.R. 6418 would require the commission to maintain standards and procedures to establish revenue levels for motor carriers that are adequate "under honest, economical, and efficient management, to cover total expenses including the operation of leased equipment, depreciation, and obsolescence, plus a reasonable profit." The commission is instructed to take into consideration the goal that carriers achieve adequate revenue levels and take into account reasonable estimated or foreseeable future costs. The Senate bill contains comparable language.

Other Provisions. H.R. 6418 would make many of the additional substantial changes included in the Senate bill, though it omits lengthy provisions on truck safety, enlarged tonnage haulage by agricultural cooperatives for other than itself and members, and provision for a study commission. It includes a prohibition against discriminatory taxation of motor carrier transportation property employed in interstate commerce that is not found in the Senate bill.

Other Bills

Among the bills before the Congress are the following illustrative of differing approaches to the regulation of motor carrier transportation of property. Because these bills do not appear to be the prime subjects of congressional attention, only the principal features will be outlined.

S. 1496. The Motor Carrier Regulation Improvement Act of 1979 was introduced by Senator Daniel K. Inouye (D-Hawaii) at the request of the American Trucking Associations. This bill endorses the plan of regulation adopted in 1935. It would retain the existing entry criteria requiring that the applicant be fit, willing, and able and that the transportation proposed is or will be required by public convenience and necessity. The applicant would continue to have the burden of proof.

The ICC would have to make specific findings on certain issues in connection with an entry application, including the effect entry would have on existing carriers, effect on the energy efficiency of existing carriers, and so forth. The ICC would have to make findings on reasonable broadening of commodity categories where the public's need for this has been demonstrated to the ICC. Circuitous routing could be removed if the applicant carrier demonstrates to the ICC that such routing wastes fuel and is inefficient, and that a need for change exists.

The ICC would not consider the level of rates in making these specific findings unless the rates are so high as to constitute an embargo on traffic. The class of persons that may contest an application would be narrowed. The "rule of eight" for contract carriers would be eliminated and operations could not be limited to a particular industry or geographical area for such a carrier. Private carriers exempt from regulation because they are primarily engaged in business other than transportation could not be certificated as contract carriers or common carriers.

Intercorporate hauling would be dealt with as in the Senate bill. Trucking movement of air traffic on a through ticket or through bill of lading would be limited to thirty-five miles of the airport or airport city, but an advance of freight charges by the airline or freight forwarder would be prima facie evidence that the carrier by truck was not a bona fide agent. Motor carriage could be substituted for air carriage if performed at the expense of the air carrier or freight forwarder on a through air bill of lading and if this were necessitated by emergency conditions due to adverse weather, equipment failure, or other causes beyond the control of the airline.

The ICC would have to approve rate bureau agreements unless they violated some provision of the statute on rate bureau activities or unless the agreements would not further national transportation policy. The ICC could require conditions to such agreements to ensure a uniform rate structure for reasonably related rates and charges. The antitrust laws would not apply to those making or carrying out approved rate bureau agreements. A carrier could vote on rates and so forth if it were legally authorized to transport any of the commodities to which the proposal applied. But if the agreement for the rate bureau provides for a democratically constituted representative committee of carriers, the members of the committee could vote even though some may not be legally authorized to haul the commodities involved. No distinction would be made between single-line and joint-line rates. A carrier's right of independent action would be protected and other reforms would be adopted. The ICC would be required to approve and maintain rate levels that are adequate to cover operating expenses plus a reasonable profit and so forth, as provided in the Senate bill.

The zone of rate freedom would permit increases or decreases of 7 percent as compared with rates effective a year before but decreases would be subject to suspension by the ICC if they involved a practice that is unfair, destructive, or predatory, or otherwise undermines competition.

The bill would permit the ICC to set intrastate rates, adjusting those rates to the interstate rates charged for similar traffic, if the state regulatory authority fails to act finally on a proposed change in intrastate rates within 120 days of their filing. The prohibition against state and local tax discrimination involving motor carrier transportation property is the same as in H.R. 6418. Provisions are included to require expedited action by the ICC.

S. 1497. This bill, entitled the Motor Carrier Efficiency and Regulatory Improvement Act of 1979, was introduced by Senator Inouye at the request of the Teamsters Union. Congressional findings in the bill would require the ICC to accord carriers reasonable rate flexibility and encourage the provision of fair wages and healthy working conditions for carriers' employees. It would not permit compensated haulage by separate but affiliated companies of a private carrier to be exempt from regulation.

Entry criteria would be as in S. 1496 except for the omission of language on broadening commodity categories and removal of circuitous route restrictions. Lower rates could not be the sole or principal basis for a grant of entry. Common carriers would have to actually provide the service required by the certificate approved by the ICC and render reasonably continuous, safe, and adequate service to the public. Failure to do so would be grounds for suspension or revocation of the certificate. In considering the grant of a certificate the ICC would have to consider the energy efficiency of the proposed service and its effect on highway safety. A private carrier could not be certificated as a common carrier or contract carrier.

The rate bureau provisions of this bill are the same as in S. 1496 except for three additions. The rate standards adopted by the ICC must cover payment of fair wages and benefits to employees of carriers; determination of a reasonable rate of return must not be based solely or primarily on carrier return on investment or equity; and rate levels must not directly or indirectly harm carriers who are parties to collective bargaining agreements or the wages and fringe benefits of employees that are contained in such collective bargaining agreements.

The zone of rate freedom would be the same as in S. 1496 except the yearly increase in limits would not exceed either 7 percent or the increase in the consumer price index for urban wage earners and clerical workers, whichever is greater.

The ICC would have to require that the driver of a leased vehicle hauling property for a carrier be an employee of the carrier when safety of operations, control, and responsibility of the carrier for the driver will be improved by an employer-employee relationship.

4

Major Issues Involving Legislative Change

The key provisions of the bills described above are central to the regulatory reform debate that has been ongoing since the motor carrier regulations were first imposed. This debate was heightened with the proposals first introduced in the Congress and advanced by the administration in 1971.[11] The initial stimulus for these bills was the collapse of the Penn Central Railroad in 1970. Early reform proposals recommended the overhaul of the entire regulated transportation sector, including railroads, motor carriers, and water carriers. Certain railroad regulatory changes were enacted in 1976, under the so-called "4R" Act, but no significant legislative changes have been made in motor carrier regulation.

The controversy over change in the motor carrier regulatory scheme stems from conflicting sets of philosophies as the variety of approaches contained in pending bills demonstrates. The principal arguments of those favoring regulatory change and those opposed are summarized below.

Arguments of Proponents for Change

Generally, those who press for change in the regulatory structure believe that current regulations seriously misallocate industry's resources, hamper managerial innovation, and interfere with the efficiencies of the better managed operating firms. They also argue that the cartel-like operation of the rate bureaus, rate regulation favorable to the least efficient carriers, ICC barriers to new entrants, and restrictions on innovations by those already in the industry make the industry sluggish and increasingly concentrated.

Proponents argue further that those who enjoy the benefits of regulation also enjoy profits above a competitive level. Former Assistant Attorney General John H. Shenefield, in testimony on the Carter–Kennedy proposal, stated:

> For the twelve months ended June 1978, the average rate of return on equity for the eight largest trucking companies was almost 27 percent, almost double the average return on equity for all manufacturing. For the comparable period in 1979, the figure is in excess of 22 percent. In 1977, ninety-eight of the Nation's largest trucking firms earned a rate of return on equity of almost 20 percent, which prompted the ICC staff itself to acknowledge that excessive profits were being earned. The data released by Senator Kennedy last July show that concentration in the general freight sector in individual

city-pair markets is extremely high, with the top four carriers accounting for 62 to 64 percent of the average, and with ratios in very many cases ranging between 70 and 90 percent. The only interpretation that common sense will allow of the trucking industry's vehement opposition to S. 1400 is that regulation in its present form is good for piling up excessive bottom line profits.[12]

The United States Justice Department also points to stock market anaiysts, who have for years counted on ICC restrictions as a boon for insured profitability of the largest motor carriers. Proponents argue that the foregoing conditions contribute to intolerable profit ranges in a time of double-digit inflation. President Carter, in submitting the administration's legislative proposal, estimated that the changes brought about by that bill would save consumers $5 billion annually in reduced shipping costs. A Congressional Budget Office report estimated that deregulation could save $5 billion to $8 billion a year.[13]

Proponents also point to ICC restrictions on routing and on the commodities that may be carried as wasteful of badly needed petroleum resources. Gateway restrictions alone are estimated to cost $141 million, to cause a loss of 51 million gallons of fuel, and to cost ten lives a year.[14] Restrictions on backhauls also waste energy, reform proponents say. A 1976 General Accounting Office study reported that 20.4 percent of all trucks now hauling agricultural commodities were traveling empty one way.[15]

In answer to claims that "chaos" will occur in the transportation market with disruptive and injurious competition, that carriers will concentrate on lucrative markets at the expense of small communities, and that highway safety will suffer with the entry of more accident-prone independent truckers, proponents point to the fact that it is the Department of Transportation that regulates traffic safety for motor carriers at the federal level, not the ICC; that only 40 percent of the commodities carried on the highways are carried by regulated carriers and the carriers of the other 60 percent have a satisfactory safety record by comparison; and that airlines have survived such cutbacks in regulation without injury to their safety record. They also point to even more dramatic results from "deregulation" in Canada, Great Britain, and Austria.[16]

Those seeking regulatory change argue that small communities are now being served "in spite of, not because of" existing regulation.[17] A study prepared for the Department of Transportation concluded that:

> The results of this study indicate that the motor common carrier system is not important in maintaining the viability of small communities in isolated areas. Two major findings lead to this conclusion:
>
> 1. Although the common carrier service obligations require carriers to serve all points in their operating certificates, common carriers in the current regulated environment are able to avoid

serving small towns in isolated areas if they consider such traffic to be unprofitable (i.e., the cross-subsidization argument has no empirical support).

2. Communities are being served by other types of interstate carriers (UPS, private carriers, short-haul interstate carriers, bus package service) and when all the various types of carriers are considered, the overall level of service is adequate to meet the needs of the communities.[18]

Proponents of change also argue that ICC restrictions on entry and service expansion also most severely affect small businesses (shippers and truckers) and minority groups seeking to enter the market or enlarge their operations.[19]

Arguments of Opponents of Change

Those who oppose regulatory change in the motor carrier field start with the proposition that the regulatory system as now designed has served the nation well. It has provided security for the essential common carrier system upon which the nation's shippers rely. It has grown, they claim, to serve the needs of communities and of shippers both large and small. Regulated trucking, unlike the railroad industry, is not on the brink of financial disaster but is functioning well, opponents say. A spokesman for the American Trucking Associations remarked: "The system is working pretty well. We've been saying, 'If it's not broke, don't fix it.'"[20] Opponents argue that to eliminate existing regulatory controls would undermine the strength of the common carrier system and would inject destructive competition, weaken the carriers, and injure shippers and communities by the possible collapse of the industry. Small communities might be left without service or might be required to pay excessive prices for any service.[21]

Opponents contend that tinkering with the system will destroy the notion of a common carrier obligation to offer service on a nondiscriminatory basis to all shippers according to published tariffs. Pirate operators would enter the more desirable trucking markets and "skim the cream" of more profitable traffic, leaving the less profitable traffic to the general common carrier. A corollary argument is that transportation of certain low-value commodities is unprofitable and—if the commodities are to be shipped—they require cross-subsidization from other traffic movements. Small communities would likewise lose service unless they were cross-subsidized, opponents argue.

Regulatory change, it is argued, would also result in even greater concentration in the industry as the larger carriers with greater financial reserves and broader markets would be in a position to take over less fortunate carriers, or smaller carriers would simply drop by the wayside, in the same fashion as stock brokerage firms did after brokerage rates were "deregulated."

Without stringent rate regulation by the ICC, according to opponents, rates may be set unreasonably high or unreasonably low. Certain carriers serving "captive" shippers could raise their rates to monopoly price levels. On the down side, a large carrier with enough income from other markets could drop his rate to a predatory level to drive out other carriers and then raise it to monopoly levels once the shippers are "captive."

Existing rate regulation and the antitrust exemption for rate bureaus also contributes to rate stability and predictability, opponents argue. With rate freedom and without the tempering of rate actions by group decision within a rate bureau, rates would fluctuate in extremes. Also, without rate bureaus, rates could not be published, leaving shippers in the dark as to what they would be paying and what their competitors are paying. Also, it is alleged, carriers could not agree on interline or joint rates in absence of antitrust immunity and carriers could not agree on a standard set of classifications for commodities or mileages.

According to the American Trucking Associations:

> *Collective ratemaking is plainly and simply a benefit to the shippers and actually reduces the cost of truck transportation.* Shipper organizations such as the National Industrial Traffic League and the National Small Shipments Traffic Conference have voiced their strong support for continued collective rate making in testimony before the Senate Commerce Committee.
>
> One might say that collective ratemaking reduces the unwieldy to the manageable. Envision the hundreds of thousands of commodities, today reduced to twenty-three classification ratings, that travel among more than 125,000 points and places in the U.S. The need for some kind of stabilizing system is apparent. Without regulation thousands of separate carriers would set rates for hundreds of thousands of commodities among an untold combination of origins and destinations. Each bureau publishes the rates for each class of trucking between different points. Without collective ratemaking, a shipper would not know whether he was being charged a reasonable rate. The costs of individual rate researching would be passed on to the consumer. No shipper would know one day to the next what his shipping costs or the rates his competitors were paying would be. Truck transportation would be reduced to a lottery. . . .
>
> Repeal of the antitrust immunity for collective ratemaking will mean that traffic moving today in joint-line service will have to move at a combination of local rates—in other words, individual rates for each segment of the movement on separate bills of lading. This will be far more costly to the shipper and ultimately the consumer.[22]

Clearly, the debate is intense. In the view of the American Trucking Associations, "S. 2245 poses a major problem for the regulated trucking industry—the most important problem it has faced since the inception of regulation in 1935."[23]

National Transportation Policy. The provision of S. 2245 requiring the ICC to "promote competitive and efficient transportation services," coupled with the Senate committee's report language stating its intent that national transportation policy "must recognize the importance of competition as the most desirable means for achieving transportation goals," would indicate that at the very least the ICC is instructed to make procompetition policy one of the key elements of its regulatory decision making.

The committee stepped back from earlier language and language in the Carter–Kennedy bill requiring the commission to rely "to the maximum extent feasible upon actual and potential competition." Even this compromise, however, may not have satisfied the demands of the American Trucking Associations. Its testimony before the committee declared:

> [R]egulation in the public interest in furtherance of the vital common carrier concept is basically inconsistent with competition. Elements of regulation such as entry control and rate regulation cannot be justified if competition, unrestrained, is to be the objective. Moreover, such language, or direction, as contained in S. 2245 could be used by the present Interstate Commerce Commission to more vigorously pursue its announced intention of administrative deregulation.[24]

On the other hand, shipper groups favored the stronger, procompetitive language for precisely the reason ATA opposed. One group, CURRENT, in comments on H.R. 6418 stated: "The lack of reliance upon competitive focus as a prime element of transportation policy in prior decades has been a fundamental failing of our domestic transport regulations."[25]

Entry. As previously noted, H.R. 6418 would require that the new applicant show by a preponderance of the evidence that its entry is in the public interest; S. 2245 places the burden on opponents to show that the new entry would not be in the public interest. This is the key difference in the entry standards of the two bills.

Industry representatives have testified in strong opposition to this burden of proof provision in S. 2245 as an unwarranted reversal of time-proven procedures, charging that it would lead to excessive entry, destructive competition, overcapacity, and excessive fuel use. The witness for the American Trucking Associations testified:

> S. 2245 makes a far-reaching change in the provisions covering the granting of operating authorities. The bill provides that certificates shall be issued *unless* there is a finding that the transportation to be provided would be *inconsistent* with the present or future

public convenience and necessity. That is a negative approach and goes completely contrary to the nature and intent of findings of public convenience and necessity. The purpose of such standards in entry controls is to determine that there is a need and upon such a finding, to grant such authorities, providing other criteria are met. This provision of S. 2245 is a complete reversal of these long-standing and time-proven procedures. Under the proposed approach, certificates would be easier to obtain. This presents the real danger of excess capacity with resulting inefficiencies, particularly in fuel usage. There is no solid evidence showing that the granting of certificates should not continue to be on the basis of a positive finding that what is proposed is consistent with present or future public convenience and necessity. The provisions of S. 2245 should be changed to conform with what has proven to be necessary to achieve one of the objectives of regulation—avoidance of destructive competition by not creating a transportation supply greater than demand dictates.[26]

Senators Hollings (D-S.C.) and Inouye argue that small towns and communities will suffer the most from enactment of the pending legislation. They assert that these communities will pay the highest price through increased rates and poorer service. These senators question the conclusions of a November 30, 1979, Department of Transportation study on service to six small communities, claiming that the conclusions of staff are not justified by the actual interviews.

The senators also cite the example of a particular carrier with 230 of its 440 terminals in towns of less than 30,000 population (nearly 100 in towns of less than 10,000). They say that such carriers need a balance of truckload and less-than-truckload shipments to continue service to such communities. They contend that, with free entry, other carriers would seek to skim off the more profitable truckload shipments and the carrier cited could not then afford to continue handling less-than-truckload shipments at prior rates. The result, according to the senators, would be that the carrier would charge more for less-than-truckload shipments to and from such communities and would have extra unnecessary miles of empty backhaul.

Because nearly 40,000 of the 61,000 communities in the United States are completely dependent on motor carriers for freight service, the senators contend that substantially open entry would frustrate continued enjoyment of national transportation policy objectives of safe, adequate, economical, and efficient motor carrier service without unjust discrimination, undue preference or advantages, or unfair or destructive competitive practices. Indiscriminate allowance of entry would, in their view, result in the creation of more transportation than is required by demand, waste of fuel, and risk to highway safety. Smaller trucking firms might fail with greater concentration of business in a few large firms. They contend that unrestricted competition and fulfillment of the common carrier obligation are incompatible.[27]

Shippers—with several exceptions—and consumer groups favor relaxation of entry controls.[28] Proponents of freer entry policies contend the current application process is an expensive, time-consuming, and often futile procedure. The chairman of the ICC has stated that the commission has a backlog of 20,000 applications and each application takes an average of ten months for processing. Thus, many carriers find that the easiest way to get into the trucking business is to purchase the operating rights of an existing carrier.

Even this avenue of entry can be quite expensive. Thus, when Associated Transport, Inc., went bankrupt in 1976, its operating rights, carried on its books at $1 million, sold for $20 million. Small operators and minority-owned firms, it is argued, simply cannot secure entry to lucrative routes because of the difficulty of entry in competition with carriers with grandfather rights, and small operators cannot afford to enter by purchase of expensive operating rights.

Proponents of deregulation and freer entry claim that what is needed is a healthy dose of competition to drive down rates. Control of entry, according to reform proponents, protects inefficient carriers. Competition, they claim, produces dynamism; carriers will take risks if they see the opportunity to win a greater share of the market and obtain the financial rewards obviously available in a field in which carriers are said to be earning a 20 percent rate of return. Advocates of competition argue that carriers should compete with quality of management and with better prices and services rather than on the basis of the quality of their transportation counsel and the disposition of bureaucrats in Washington.

Regulation, in their view, is the biggest obstacle to better and expanded service to small communities. Currently the ICC freely grants applications to drop service to small communities and fails to enforce the common carrier obligation of other firms that simply fail to provide service in accordance with their operating rights, but refusal of new entry denies these communities the services they are entitled to.[29]

Critics of freer entry, such as Frank Fitzsimmons, president of the Teamsters Union, argue that "the mindless competition resulting from unrestrained entry of independents who don't know their costs would be destructive of our truck transportation system."[30] The volume of goods to be carried is relatively fixed, it is claimed, and freer entry would simply mean that more truckers would be chasing the same amount of business with great waste of scarce fuel. Freer entry, it is claimed, would mean more empty backhauls rather than fewer.

Allowing more trucking companies to compete will simply mean, according to critics, that many small truckers will be put out of business because of needless competition with greater rather than less concentration in the trucking business. The independent truckers who would be let into the regulated market by a policy of freer entry are those who have the worst record for accidents, speeding, long overtime hours, and false logging, according to opponents of reform.

Regulated common carriers would have less incentive to serve small communities, opponents argue, because they could not protect such service areas for themselves by providing adequate and responsive service. Common carriers, it is claimed, are like public utilities, but they cannot continue to perform as public utilities if unlimited numbers of operators can enter the market.

Some minority-group leaders argue freer entry is of no help to minority businesses unless the economy is growing, for these businesses have little chance to compete when the size of the economic pie is shrinking. Some critics claim that it is unfair to open the gates to a flood of new competition because this will result in a capital loss of as much as $5 billion in the value of operating rights. This, it is asserted, is unfair and will be a particular blow to companies that have purchased such rights for large sums of money.[31]

Proponents of freer entry respond that regulated carriers have too often neglected their obligations to serve small communities. With free exit from those markets and no ICC enforcement of a service requirement, they say, there is no public utility-type relationship worth preserving.

In their view, there are few economies of scale in the trucking business and costs are variable. As a result, it makes sense to remove regulations that set and preserve rates at levels high enough to protect the least efficient operators. Some of the least efficient may be forced out, but the operator who feels he can provide better or less expensive service should have the opportunity. The shipping and consuming public will gain the benefit of lower rates, an important initiative in fighting inflation.

So far as operating rights are concerned, proponents of freer entry claim that those who purchase such rights took a normal business risk and should not be protected from competition or bailed out by public purchase of their operating rights. These operators do have a significant head start over any new competition, and competition will build gradually, it is claimed, so they should be able to compete if they provide good service at reasonable rates. In any event freer entry has been discussed for the past several years, and proponents argue operating rights are already discounted in value because of this. Senator Cannon argues that freer entry is essential to offset the greater freedom that truckers will have to raise rates. He contends that only the threat of competition from new firms can restrain truckers from taking the maximum increase in rates permitted by the proposed legislation. Senator Packwood rejects the claim that small trucking firms will be absorbed by larger firms, thus producing greater concentration. If that were true, he contends, small firms would oppose and large firms would favor deregulation, but the opposite is said to be true.[32]

Proponents and opponents of trucking regulatory reform draw opposite conclusions from experience with air deregulation on service to smaller communities. Opponents charge that twenty-five small cities have lost air service since deregulation. The chairman of the Civil Aeronautics Board claims that only one has lost service, and it preferred service through a nearby city. The chairman also argued that many more cities lost air service before airline deregulation than after. Supporters of deregulation cite studies by the ICC and the Congressional Budget Office to show that many truckers polled indicated they would continue to serve small communities and that non-regulated carriers have been providing most of the service to these communities in any event.[33]

Removal of Operating Restrictions. Current regulatory practices have led to a series of restrictions that critics contend cause poor utilization of equipment and inflated transportation costs for users of transportation services. Operating certificates often contain narrow territorial operating restrictions, narrow limitations on the commodities that may be hauled, and restrictions that limit trucking to one-way hauls and prevent the backhaul of other commodities. Many certificates also prohibit a trucker from serving intermediate points between cities. Routes that have been extended by tacking together two or more authorities may require entry by a circuitous route—so-called gateway restrictions.

Secretary of Transportation Goldschmidt argued that removal of these restrictions could save 220 million to 330 million gallons of gasoline a year. The ICC estimates that 5 percent of all interlined traffic could be handled directly as intermediate stops along regular routes and that this could save up to 1.9 million gallons of fuel annually. Thus, it is claimed that prohibiting intermediate stops prevents regulated carriers from serving small communities.[34]

Provisions of S. 2245 instruct the ICC to eliminate, within 180 days, gateway and circuitous route restrictions. Other restrictions on commodities, interim point limitations, and those that are wasteful or inefficient are to be dealt with on a case-by-case basis. H.R. 6418 requires that all removal of such restrictions be dealt with in individual cases. This case-by-case approach has been criticized by proponents of liberalized entry as encouraging excessive litigation, expense to the parties, and regulatory lag.[35]

The overall objectives of eliminating most operating restrictions are applauded by the same groups, however.

The industry, in testimony before the House and Senate Committees strongly supported the case-by-case approach:

> The motor carrier industry is opposed to an across-the-board elimination of all gateway and circuity restrictions as provided for in S. 2245. Since the elimination of such restrictions are directed toward improving carrier efficiencies, and in particular energy efficiency, we believe that the best approach is to provide for an expedited procedure under which such restrictions can be eliminated on a case-by-case basis.[36]

On the removal of interim point limitations, the motor carriers argue that the "short-haul" local carrier could be destroyed without regulatory protection.

> The local and short-haul carrier is often the connecting link between regular-route line-haul carriers and small communities. Without their interline and pooling services, the movement of "small shipments" to and from many of these communities would be made much more difficult. There is a delicate balance in the cooperative as well as competitive relationship between the typical regular-route line-haul carrier and the local and short-haul consolidation-distribution carrier. Each competes with but relies upon the other. More importantly, however, small and remote communities served exclusively by the short-haul carrier depend on the cooperative relationship for their long-haul service. A perusal of any Rand-McNally reveals that "intermediate and off-route" points are most often remote points of scant population. Accordingly, such points are seldom marked by significant commercial activity sufficient to support, or even attract, an abundance of competitive motor carriers. The service which is provided, especially at "off-route points," is only provided in conjunction with service to other points.[37]

The American Trucking Associations also opposes generalized broadening of the list of commodities carriers are authorized to handle, stating:

> In addition, S. 2245 would cause to be implemented regulations which would broaden the categories of commodities authorized by a carrier's certificate. To do so without first specifically requiring of each applicant a demonstration of public need, both undermines and emasculates consideration of energy consumption, potential cost savings and improved efficiency, as well as the transportation policy, which the commission will be required to consider. As with the elimination of gateway restrictions and circuitous route limitations, the effect will be to permit the commission to rubber-stamp all applications without any valid consideration of the specific concerns of Congress.[38]

Additional Exemptions. The Senate bill has gone further in exempting new categories of agricultural foodstuffs (whether processed or not) and supplies, and has drawn the most criticism from the American Trucking Associations, the Association of American Railroads, and the National Meat Association.

The National Meat Association is concerned that the food exemption "will lead to greater difficulty in securing an adequate number of refrigerated trucks to economically move America's meat supply."[39]

Other shippers, now within the present exemption, have expressed concern that extending the exemption to processed food products could reduce the number of trucks available to haul shipments already exempt.[40]

The associations of motor carriers and railroads object to the extension of the agricultural exemption on the ground that it would divert traffic of the new commodities to the exempt carriers away from regulated rail and motor carriers. The American Trucking Associations is currently supporting an amendment to delete processed foods from an expanded agricultural exemption.

The Association of American Railroads, in opposing the broadened agricultural exemption, stated:

> Today, it is the railroads which, alone, operate as common carriers under almost complete economic regulation. Only a little more than 40 percent of the motor carrier industry is regulated. Almost no water carrier operations are subject to ICC review. Any legislation which would serve to worsen this already inequitable situation should be considered only after steps are taken to deregulate the railroad industry in a significant way.[41]

Senators Hollings and Inouye contend that the greatest danger to the common carrier system lies in the uncontrolled growth of exempt for-hire transportation. They argue that the committee's agricultural exemption is so broad that it would erode the operating base of regulated carriers. In their view adding processed food to the exempt list will make the current problems of the agricultural community worse by luring truckers who currently move unprocessed products from farm to market into making nonagricultural intercity hauls of processed food products. Such hauls offer balanced hauls to more desirable areas of the country. These senators contend that expanding the agricultural exemption to processed food products would not eliminate empty backhauls; it would simply shift empty miles from one carrier to another. Such backhauls, they contend, are more the result of a natural imbalance of products to be hauled and of the limited flexibility of trucking equipment (auto transports, for example, can only haul autos). The original rationale for the current, more limited agricultural commodity exemption lies in the perishable nature of many commodities and the seasonal need for transportation by a large number of vehicles for a short period of time. Senators Hollings and Inouye contend that this rationale does not extend to processed agricultural commodities, as was recognized at the time of enactment of the original exemption.[42]

Senators Hollings and Inouye echo the criticism of rail carriers when they argue that the broadened exemption would worsen the plight of the railroads. Regulated rail and truck carriers, they claim, now transport 230 million tons or 64 percent of all processed food and agricultural chemicals. Loss of this tonnage or a substantial part of it would be a serious blow to these carriers. It is said that regulated truck carriers stand to lose 89 million tons that brought them $4 billion in revenues in 1979.

These senators claim that regulation has in fact kept commodity rates low, so that consumers are unlikely to benefit from lower prices as a result of an enlarged agricultural commodities exemption. Unregulated carriers who would enter the field of transportation for processed agricultural commodities are, in the view of the senators, less reliable and more accident-prone. As a result, the food distribution system will deteriorate and become less reliable if these truckers participate. In their view the competitive position of the ailing railroad industry as against trucking would deteriorate.[43]

Senators Hollings and Inouye also criticize the provision in S. 2245 as reported by the committee that would exempt motor carrier transportation incident to prior or subsequent rail haulage from regulation. They argue that rail-affiliated motor carriers and their rail parents or mutual holding companies could use joint rail-trucking services to eliminate competition and increase their market share. Nonaffiliated motor carriers would be unable to compete, in their view, and would be forced out of the market. Because railroad carriage has not been deregulated, the senators claim the pending bill would make joint rail-trucking carriage half regulated and half deregulated. They say that the provision of the Senate bill requiring motor carriers to enter into joint-rate and through-route agreements with railroads is inconsistent with the unregulated status of the motor carrier portion of joint haul traffic. Indeed, they say, this provision would deregulate the motor carrier haulage of hazardous materials. This provision was deleted during Senate debate on a motion of Senator Cannon, the committee chairman.[44]

Senators Hollings and Inouye also object to exempting carriers of shipments of 100 pounds or less from regulation. They note that such shipments make up 15 percent of the regulated trucking market, too great a portion if entry control is to be maintained. They contend there is no justification in the hearing record for this change. They note that new entrants will not be required to demonstrate a need for their services but can seek to capture the most profitable small package transportation markets, and that this will harm many small carriers and shippers.[45]

The American Farm Bureau, on the other hand, favors expansion of the agricultural exemption.

> [W]e would deregulate specifically uncooked meat, and with the present price of meat in this country, consumers ought to be a little bit interested in that, and just for good measure, we'd throw in bananas. We would then expand the exemption to include the major agricultural production input items—these are the items that farmers have to purchase in order to carry on their production. And they are items that generally move in the opposite direction from the agricultural commodities that leave the farm. They move generally from east to west and from north to south, and the agricultural commodities move generally from south to north and from west to east.[46]

The National Council of Farmer Cooperatives favors liberalizing agricultural exemptions to include processed foods and farm supplies:

> While the agricultural exemption has been of great benefit to rural shippers, its potential is significantly unrealized because, like the agricultural cooperative truckers, the exempt haulers face substantial backhaul problems. Produce moving from the rural areas to the cities is exempt. Input items moving from manufacturing centers to the farms are tightly regulated. This means that the many carriers meeting rural transportation needs must either return empty or contract their services to a carrier with a certificate covering the movement of nonexempt items to a particular small community at terms dictated by the certified carrier. This forces the exempt carrier to cover a disproportionate share of his costs on the outbound move, driving up food prices and/or lowering farm income.
>
> Exempting all food from regulation would remove incongruities from the existing law, improve service and lower rates for food processors, encourage the location of processing facilities in rural areas near sources of supply, and help hold down food costs at all regions of the country.[47]

The majority of the Senate Committee on Commerce, Science and Transportation voted to expand the agricultural exemption to include all food items, whether processed or not, and certain other items such as soil conditioners and nonhazardous agricultural chemicals and fertilizers. The majority explained that the current law requires many arbitrary decisions as to what are or are not unprocessed food commodities and that these artificial distinctions would be avoided by the broader exemption. Senator Cannon claims the change would help avoid energy waste, because exempt carriers run empty 28 percent of the time now as a result of current government regulatory restrictions. Some 70 percent of the processed foods are now carried by private carriers rather than regulated carriers, demonstrating, in the view of the committee majority, that regulated carriers are not meeting shippers' needs in this area. Processed food, in the view of the committee majority, accounts for only about 4 percent of the total motor carrier transportation market in both tonnage and revenues, so truckers will not lose large revenues. Because regulated carriers do in fact carry exempt commodities now, they can be expected to share in the carriage of newly exempt commodities as well.

The committee majority defended exemption of trucking preceding or following rail shipment as an extension of existing authority to deliver and pick up items for rail transit within rail terminal zones. The committee majority and Senator Adlai E. Stevenson III (D-Ill.), the author of the committee amendment, argue that this will be of particular benefit to the transportation of items moving by rail in truck trailers loaded on rail flatcars.[48]

The major argument advanced for exemption of processed food products is that when truck movement of fresh and frozen fruits and vegetables was exempted from ICC regulation in the 1950s, transportation rates for these commodities dropped 33 percent on poultry and 19 percent on fruits and vegetables, according to estimates of the Agriculture Department.[49]

Rate Flexibility. A consensus is growing that strict ICC powers over the rates carriers may charge should be loosened. The principal bills would permit upward and downward variation of rates by a significant percentage. Within the zone of rate freedom, the ICC could not challenge rates as unusually high or low though it could suspend and investigate discriminatory and predatory rates. The Senate version would require that rate-setting freedom within the stated range be keyed to removal of collective rate making—that individual carriers be free to make their own pricing choices.

The arguments for carrier management determination of rates, rather than regulatory rulings, as the basis for pricing of transportation services have long been advanced. Operating companies, it is argued, should have flexibility in making pricing decisions and in innovating price packages tailored to shipper needs. Experience in Canada is claimed to demonstrate that with rate freedom shippers are more responsive to shippers' needs. In addition, proponents of the zone of rate freedom system argue that carrier freedom to set rates will permit rates which would more nearly approximate the cost of providing the transportation. Proponents also argue that the requirement that a carrier focus on individual costs will make management more conscious of the particular cost structures a company may face, and it will devise further efficiencies in delivery of services. The majority of the Senate committee favoring S. 2245 argued that allowing freer entry would not achieve the economies and efficiencies desired if truckers did not have freedom to compete as to price.[50]

Pricing freedom on the part of motor carriers brings with it several concerns on the part of some shippers. Shippers have been protected in the past by laws barring discrimination in prices one shipper may pay as against another; carriers have also been protected from predatory pricing from other larger carriers. The American Trucking Associations has supported a defined zone of freedom but suggests that any such zone be subject to the power of the commission to suspend and investigate discrimination or predatory pricing practices inherent in carrier rates.[51] That power would remain under the pending bills, and carriers who make unlawful rebates are subject to criminal sanctions under current law. Shippers receiving such rebates may be prosecuted and sued for damages totaling three times the amount of the illegal rebate.[52]

Some shippers and small businesses supporting a zone of rate freedom argue that any such flexibility of pricing must be coupled with improved entry for new carriers and the elimination of antitrust immunity for collective rate making. They argue that entry freedom without flexibility of pricing and the elimination of collective rate making will only serve to push motor carrier rates to the 10 percent or other ceiling established for the zone of rate freedom.

The National Federation of Independent Business (NFIB) applauds the rights of individual carriers to set their rates within a zone of rate freedom. "However, this allowance of individual rate setting will cause a terrible result if not accompanied by a strong free entry section in [the legislation]." With such rate flexibility, NFIB argues, "If there are not new entrants ready to compete for traffic with lower prices, the traffic will have to bear a maximum rate increase." Moreover,

> Carriers should not be allowed to collectively fix rates within the zone. Such a situation would inhibit individual carriers from setting different rates as well as possibly circumscribe the ICC's ability to scrutinize the rate making activity.[53]

Some proponents of greater carrier freedom to set rates contend that the ICC has not really set rate-of-return on carriers as is true of public utilities, nor has it imposed formal efficiency standards. These proponents argue that if motor carriers are to continue to enjoy entry restrictions and collective rate setting—which these proponents regard as collusive price fixing—the public should be protected from monopoly profits by strong rate-of-return regulation and formal efficiency standards.[54]

Senators Hollings and Inouye contend, on the other hand, that the heart of the finest transportation system in the world is the American trucking industry. They argue that removal of regulation will return the industry to the conditions that led to regulation initially, namely, inequality of rates, and unequal and prejudicial treatment as to persons, places, and property. In their view large shippers, because of their large freight volume and financial position, would be able to obtain special rates, concessions, and preferences. That, they note, is prohibited under current law.[55]

On the other side it is argued that the law prohibits discrimination. In any event, if cost differentials are not justified, carriers thus discriminating will lose business to competing firms. Only a monopoly, it is asserted, can practice price discrimination. Price competition, in contrast, will ensure that rates are cost-based, and it is argued, it is just because many current rates are not cost-based that regulated carriers are losing business to private carriers. Claims that chaos may result are discounted by critics of regulation who insist that the unsettled conditions that preceded motor carrier regulation stemmed from the Great Depression and the participation of many small truckers seeking to make a living who preferred low earnings to unemployment. Freer entry, it is argued, will allow additional persons to start up new trucking companies, thus providing employment to more people.

Antitrust Immunity for Rate Bureau Activities. The executive branch has, since 1971, supported a rollback of antitrust immunity for certain rate bureau practices. Successive administrations have urged the Congress to eliminate antitrust immunity for horizontal rate-making agreements in the bureaus. At present, members of carrier rate bureaus may agree among themselves to set rates for single-line and joint through traffic. Under this antitrust immunity, if carrier A and carrier B agree to set a rate for traffic between Chicago and New York on their respective lines, they may, under an agreement approved by the Interstate Commerce Commission, file that rate with the commission and enjoy total immunity from antitrust prosecution for their collective rate making. The Justice Department argues that collective rate making is no more than a legalized conspiracy to set transportation charges and, if not sanctioned by the Congress, would be subject to criminal penalties under the antitrust laws.

Former Assistant Attorney General John H. Shenefield, in testimony on the Carter–Kennedy bill, stated:

> Of course, the industry euphemistically calls this behavior collective rate making, but it is nothing less than naked price-fixing—the kind of activity that in unregulated industries constitutes a felony under the Sherman Act.
>
> ICC-sanctioned price fixing is a fundamental cause of the excessive rate levels maintained in the industry. The fact is that, in the motor carrier rate bureaus, competitors jointly establish rates to maximize joint profits, just as the members of any other price-fixing cartel would do. Other regulatory controls can, and should be viewed as devices designed primarily to prop up these cartel rates, and prevent the erosion of the excess profits generated by them. Thus, entry restrictions prevent newcomers from entering easily into markets where monopoly profits are earned, and ICC rate-making authority enables rate bureau members to tie up, delay, and even prevent rate cutting by rate bureau member and non-member carriers. The simple truth is that the government—here the ICC—has all too often served not as public protector but as cartel manager—a kind of regulatory cop acting to prevent competition from breaking the cartel rate.[56]

Proponents of the elimination of antitrust immunity for collective rate making for single-line rates contend that we not only need more carriers to compete in the marketplace but we need price competition among all these carriers, old and new. Too often, it is claimed, rate bureaus average carriers' costs and set rates high enough above the average to earn a profit for the most inefficient carrier represented, thus in effect raising rates for all shippers to protect the inefficient carriers. Truckers have not resisted high wage demands, it is argued, because costs could be passed on to shippers in higher freight rates generally approved by the ICC. Single-line transportation, it is argued, tends to cost less than multi-carrier routings, yet any cost savings for single-line haulage is generally lost in collective rate making. The efficient carriers find it necessary to set rates high enough to permit less efficient (higher cost) competition to operate profitably, to gain votes for collective action.

Thus collective rate making for single-line rates is claimed to be the most anticompetitive practice of the trucking industry and a major target for reform in some of the pending bills. Phasing in the ban on collective rate making for single-line rates over three years, it is claimed, will avoid the chaos predicted by opponents. Currently, it is argued, rate bureaus base rate proposals on what they think the ICC will approve. With the changes proposed, each carrier will be under a greater compulsion to know its costs and price its services from its own point of view, thus stimulating competition and encouraging the carrier to be more efficient. Secretary Goldschmidt argues that this change could lead to cuts of 20 to 30 percent in rates in some segments of the transportation market.[57]

Proponents of change also suggest that in the long run antitrust immunity to fix rates may not benefit the carrier either. They argue that where rate-fixing agreements have existed, the industry has been saddled with overcapacity, because individual carriers seek to capture as much of the business as possible in non-price competition.

S. 2245 would eliminate antitrust immunity for single-line rate making among competitors by July 1, 1983, subject to the report of a study commission. Joint-line rate making for end-to-end movements among carriers would continue to be immune. Other joint, nonrate activities of the rate bureaus could remain exempt, such as tariff publication, traffic surveys, joint safety programs, and commodity classifications.

Those proponents who would go further than the immunity cutbacks proposed by S. 2245 argue that three years is too long a period before collective rate making for single-line rates is abolished. (The study commission could conceivably recommend legislation which would extend such joint rate making even beyond three years.) Former Assistant Attorney General Shenefield testified:

> I find it difficult to conceive what benefits are to be achieved by a three-year delay. . . . The SEC estimated that within two years after the elimination of fixed commission rates American investors saved over $700 million and that was in 1977. Since then, the savings to consumers have undoubtedly passed the $1 billion mark. We simply cannot afford *not* to eliminate antitrust immunity as soon as possible in the motor carrier industry.[58]

Supporters of more extensive cutbacks also assert that legitimate joint-line, end-to-end rate making may be accomplished without violation of the antitrust laws, and, therefore, no antitrust immunity is required. Carriers that engage in such collective rate making should do so only if they are unable to provide the entire service themselves. Under such circumstances, the carriers would enter into the relationship not as direct competitors but as each providing a service which the other could not. Proponents argue that the provision of this service and the division of revenues among the carriers would not violate the antitrust laws.

Shippers are not in universal agreement regarding the rate bureau provisions of the pending proposals. The National Industrial Traffic League would continue antitrust immunity in its present form as to single- and joint-line rate making.[59] The National Association of Manufacturers, the Grocery Manufacturers Association, and certain other shipper organizations seek to eliminate such immunity.[60] There is, however, a strong consensus of shippers favoring the "sunshine" provisions requiring open rate bureau meetings, disclosure of individual carrier votes, as well as protection of a carrier's right of of action independent from bureau protest. (Some shippers are, however, reluctant to have their operations disclosed to competitors in an open meeting.)

Senators Hollings and Inouye contend that banning collective rate making for single-line rates is inappropriate. They note that most rates are established without regard to whether transportation will be provided over a single line or a joint line, and the rates are applied simultaneously to both. Banning collective rate making for single-line rates, according to these senators, except at risk of antitrust violation, will cause most carriers to drop joint-line tariffs whenever they can move freight by single-line carriage. As a result, they say small- and medium-sized communities that now rely heavily on short-haul carriers and joint-line service will find themselves at a serious economic disadvantage. A considerable volume of traffic that formerly moved at joint-line rates will, according to these senators, be carried at local single-factor rates by a succession of truckers; each carriage will be on a separate bill of lading, at added inconvenience and cost to shippers.

The present national system of truck transportation, according to the senators, would be condemned to history. Shippers would suffer, because they would have no way of knowing what other shippers were charged and whether they themselves were being discriminated against. Senators Hollings and Inouye claim that moving motor freight at a combination of local rates, in the absence of single- and joint-line rate making, would increase shipper costs by 37 percent for a total additional cost of $1.256 billion annually.[61]

Eliminating antitrust immunity for joint rate making for single-line tariffs that account for 60 to 70 percent of regulated truck traffic, according to Senators Hollings and Inouye, would be a disadvantage to both shippers and carriers, but particularly for small carriers since joint rates permit them to compete for traffic they could not otherwise obtain. Joint rate making permits such carriers to obtain rate-setting expertise at reasonable expense and to publish and maintain required tariffs. The rate bureaus, according to the senators, have greatly simplified the publication of tariffs affecting 125,000 shipping points, hundreds of commodities, and varying rates for different weights, limitations of liability, and so forth. Thousands of small marginal trucking operators, according to the senators, could not afford to publish their own rates if collective rate making were not permitted. Without collective rate making through rate bureaus, the senators argue, shippers in turn would be saddled with the enormous cost of tracking and analyzing millions of rates. Senator Hollings argues that collective rate making is not inflationary as the ICC can verify costs and revenues semiannually and adjust rates accordingly.[62]

The strongest objections to the elimination of collective single-line rate making come from the carriers. Although they support the establishment of a study commission to determine positive and negative aspects of the current rate bureau system, they categorically oppose any cutback on collective, single-line rate making. The American Trucking Associations testified:

> In fundamental terms, if it is desirable public policy for the motor common carriers to provide a transportation network under which freight can be tendered to a carrier at any point, with a carrier obligation to accomplish the movement to destination at reasonable rates known to the shipper in advance, whether the service can be performed by the carrier alone or whether it requires a connecting carrier or carriers, the motor carriers must be permitted to participate in collective ratemaking involving joint consideration, discussion and agreement upon the rates to be submitted to the Interstate Commerce Commission for final approval. Any attempt to differentiate between single-line service performed under those rates and joint-line service performed under those rates will effectively prohibit collective ratemaking in its entirety.
>
> Collective ratemaking is necessary to the common carrier system. Without it there . . . will be no system—no network—shippers will have to find their own connecting carriers and keep track of the thousands of separate possibilities on an individual basis.[63]

Notes to Text

[1] Carole Shifrin, "The Byzantine World of Trucking Industry," *Washington Post,* March 2, 1980, p. G-1.

[2] *Congressional Record,* vol. 105 (June 25, 1979), p. S 8416, statement of Senator Edward M. Kennedy (D-Mass.).

[3] The administration's proposal was introduced as H.R. 11826 and S. 2842, 92d Congress, 1st session. If there were no effective competition from another mode of transportation, such as railroads, the upper limit of the zone of rate freedom would be set at 150 percent of fully allocated costs including a reasonable return on investment. If there were effective competition from another mode of transportation, no ceiling would be imposed on rates, because competition was expected to hold the rate line and the lower limit would be variable cost. Authority to increase and decrease rates within limits would be phased in with 15 percent variation permitted the first year and 35 percent the second.

The proposal would have removed the antitrust immunity provided by the Reed-Bulwinkle Act as to single-line rates and for carriers participating in collective rate setting for joint-line rates if they did not participate in carriage under those rates. Joint action (usually through rate bureaus) to protest or seek ICC suspension of a rate established by independent action of a carrier would also have been outside the protection of antitrust immunity. Antitrust enforcement would have been lodged with the attorney general, and private parties could proceed before the ICC to recover damages.

After a transition period, all applications for entry or for extension of service would be free from ICC disapproval on the ground of diversion of traffic from existing carriers, unless approval would result in diminution of the total quantity or quality of service available to the public. No new certificate of public convenience and necessity could prevent a carrier from altering his equipment and facilities for the routes and termini specified in the certificate. After six months the ICC could not impose limitations in new certificates as to commodities carried, points served, equipment used, routes used, and so forth to prevent diversion of traffic from an existing carrier unless failure to impose limitations would lessen service to the public. The ICC would also have to establish procedures after six months for eliminating similar restrictions in existing certificates.

[4] U.S. Department of Transportation, *Motor Carrier Reform Act,* December 1976. Because ICC suspension of rates delays their effectiveness and discourages carriers from pricing services competitively, this reform proposal would allow carriers to adjust rates freely within a gradually expanding zone of rate freedom without fear of ICC suspension. Carriers could adjust rates up or down by 7 percent the first year, 12

percent the second, 15 percent the third, and thereafter upward 15 percent per year. There would be no downward limit after the end of the third year so long as rates exceed variable costs of the specific services provided. The ICC could not suspend rates even outside the zone of rate freedom unless it were shown that a rate would result in immediate and irreparable damage. This would allow carriers to vary rates for prime hauls and backhauls and for peak and off-peak seasons and still provide protection against predatory pricing.

The bill would prohibit carrier associations from discussing, agreeing on, or voting on rates, except for the participants in joint or interline rates. After three years, rate bureau action on general rate increases would also be prohibited, though they could continue to perform administrative duties such as publishing tariffs. The bill would impose a seven- to ten-month time limit on ICC consideration of rate cases.

Entry would be facilitated by requiring the ICC to consider service to the public and the prices charged, rather than the protection of established carriers, in granting certificates. Applicants who are fit, willing, and able, and who propose rates that are compensatory and nondiscriminatory would be allowed entry. Entry procedures would be streamlined to avoid costly delays and uncertainties. The bill would remove unnecessary restrictions on entry of new contract carriers and prohibit ICC restrictions as to the number of customers they could serve or as to a particular industry or territory. Carriers could hold both a common carrier certificate and a contract carrier permit under some circumstances.

The bill sought to facilitate intermodal transportation by extending the truck zone for carriage of property on air bills of lading to 100 miles from the previous 25. The bill directed the ICC to eliminate wasteful and inefficient certificate restrictions and carriers could use direct rather than circuitous routings. Unregulated carriers of agricultural commodities could compete for carriage of regulated commodities on backhaul trips if they charged no less than the lowest available regulated rate. The bill would also allow private carriers to haul goods for their corporate subsidiaries and affiliates and to lease vehicles and drivers to regulated carriers on their return trips. Service to and from a plant less than five years old would be exempt from regulation.

[5] *Congressional Record,* vol. 125 (June 25, 1979), pp. S 8416-S 8417, remarks of Senator Kennedy on the introduction of the Carter–Kennedy bill.

[6] Ibid., vol. 126 (February 1, 1980), p. S 793.

[7] Senate Report 96-641; *Congressional Record,* vol. 126 (April 15, 1980), pp. S 3576-S 3647.

[8] Ibid., p. S 3586, statement of Senator Howard W. Cannon (D-Nev.); Senate Report 96-641, p. 5.

[9] Ibid., pp. 5-6.

[10] Private carriers are nontransportation companies that haul their own property exempt from regulation. The ICC has overturned its long-standing policy of refusing authority for private carriers to operate as common carriers or contract carriers except in exceptional circumstances. The commission was persuaded to change its policy, among other things, by the need to conserve fuel now wasted in

empty backhaul traffic by the private carriers petitioning for operating authority as regulated carriers. *Toto Purchasing and Supply Co., Inc., Common Carrier Application,* No. MC-141414 (Sub No. 1), decided by the ICC March 10, 1978. Approval of such applications is subject to the carrier's agreement to conduct its for-hire motor carrier activities and its other activities independently and to maintain separate records for each.

[11] H.R. 11826 and S. 2842, 92d Congress, 1st session.

[12] U.S. Congress, Senate, Committee on Commerce, Science and Transportation, *Hearing on Trucking Deregulation,* 96th Congress, 2d session, February 26, 1980, statement of John H. Shenefield.

[13] Remarks of Joe Sims, deputy assistant attorney general for the Antitrust Division of the Department of Justice before the forty-ninth Annual Meeting of the Association of ICC Practitioners, June 22, 1978; "Trucking: Trucking Association Attacks CBO Report as Misleading, Inaccurate," *Bureau of National Affairs Daily Report for Executives* (hereafter *BNA DER*), April 9, 1980, p. A-10.

[14] U.S. Congress, Senate and House of Representatives, Senate Committee on Commerce, Science and Transportation, House Committee on Public Works and Transportation, Subcommittee on Surface Transportation, *Joint Hearings on Trucking Deregulation,* 95th Congress, 1st session, November 17, 1979, statement of Richard A. Warren National Association of Manufacturers; see also *Petition of U.S. Department of Justice to the ICC to Eliminate Motor Carrier Gateway Restrictions on a Gradual Basis,* August 24, 1977.

[15] ICC, Bureau of Economics and Bureau of Operations, *Empty-Loaded Truck Miles on Interstate Highways during 1976,* 1977.

[16] See, for example, Thomas Gale Moore, *Trucking Regulation: Lessons from Europe* (Washington, D.C.: American Enterprise Institute, 1976).

[17] American Conservative Union, *Positive Paper,* March 1980.

[18] Department of Transportation, *Common Carrier Obligations and the Provision of Motor Carrier Service to Small Rural Communities,* July 1979, p. 123. Eleven studies of service to small communities were cited in the Senate debate. *Congressional Record,* vol. 126 (April 15, 1980), p. S 3598.

[19] U.S. Congress, House of Representatives, Committee on Public Works and Transportation, Subcommittee on Surface Transportation, *Hearings on Trucking Deregulation,* 96th Congress, 2d session, February 21, 1980, statement of Frank S. Swain, National Federation of Independent Business; remarks of William B. Hall, president of Minority Trucking Representatives Development Corporation before the Transportation Consumer Action Project Symposium, May 17, 1979.

[20] Judy Sarasohn, "Trucking Deregulation Plans Progress," *Congressional Quarterly,* vol. 38 (February 23, 1980), p. 582, quoting George Mead, legislative representative of the American Trucking Associations.

[21] Remarks of Edward V. Kiley, assistant to the president of the American Trucking Associations, before the Transportation Consumer Action Project Symposium, May 17, 1979.

[22] American Trucking Associations, *Position Paper,* undated.

[23] Ibid.

[24] *1980 Senate Hearings on Trucking Deregulation,* statement of the American Trucking Associations on S. 2245, February 27, 1980.

[25] *1980 House Hearings on Trucking Deregulation,* February 26, 1980, testimony.

[26] Ibid.

[27] Senate Report 96-641, pp. 83-86. *Congressional Record,* vol. 126 (April 15, 1980), p. S 3637, statement of Senator John A. Durkin (D-N.H.).

[28] See, for example, letter from David Cohen, president of Common Cause, to Representative Paul Simon (D-Ill.), August 10, 1979.

[29] "Trucking: Industry Efforts to Weaken Deregulation Bill Fail in Senate Committee," *BNA DER,* March 6, 1980, pp. A-11, A-12, quoting Darius W. Gaskins, chairman of the Interstate Commerce Commission as to pending motor carrier applications; "Trucking: Administration Supporting Sen. Cannon's Deregulation Bill," *BNA DER,* February 26, 1980, pp. A-10, A-11, quoting Neil Goldschmidt, secretary of transportation; "Trucking: Adm'n Officials See Regulatory Reform as the Way to Control Inflation, Energy Waste," *BNA DER,* January 17, 1980, pp. A-2, A-3, quoting Neil Goldschmidt; Shifrin, "The Byzantine World of Trucking Industry," pp. G-1, G-3; Carole Shifrin, "Deregulation on Its Way for Interstate Truckers," *Washington Post,* March 16, 1980, pp. G-1, G-3; Edward M. Kennedy, "Trucking Competition and Safety Act of 1979," *Congressional Record,* vol. 125 (June 25, 1979), pp. S 8416-S 8417; Ron Paul, "Trucking Deregulation," *Congressional Record,* vol. 125 (March 7, 1979), pp. E 962-E 963; Steven D. Symms, "Deregulation of Trucking," *Congressional Record,* vol. 125 (April 2, 1979), pp. E 1452-E 1453; "Trucking Deregulation Rolling," *Business Week,* December 5, 1977, pp. 100, 102.

[30] "Trucking: Administration Supporting Sen. Cannon's Deregulation Bill," p. A-11, quoting Fitzsimmons. Teamsters fear that up to 450,000 members might lose their jobs because of trucking regulatory reform. Judy Sarasohn, "Senate Panel Sends Trucking Bill to Floor," *Congressional Quarterly,* vol. 38 (March 15, 1980), p. 754.

[31] Ibid., p. A-11, quoting James Jesinski, secretary-treasurer of the Teamsters Union and Fitzsimmons; "Trucking Deregulation: Rolling," p. 102; "Trucking: Industry Efforts to Weaken Deregulation Bill Fail," p. A-12; "Trucking," *BNA DER,* June 5, 1979, p. A-8, quoting Representative Augustus F. Hawkins (D-Calif.), "Trucking," *BNA DER,* September 7, 1979, p. A-5, quoting Bennett C. Whitlock, president of ATA.

[32] "Trucking Deregulation: Rolling," p. 102; Symms, "Deregulation of Trucking," p. E 1453; "Trucking: Industry Efforts to Weaken Deregulation Bill Fail in Senate Committee," p. A-11, quoting Senator Cannon; *Congressional Record,* vol. 126 (April 15, 1980), p. S 3592, statement of Senator Packwood. Senator Packwood admits that the ICC grants 95 percent of all applications for operating authority but contends only 7 percent of these are for new carriers.

[33] "Airlines," *BNA DER,* March 10, 1980, p. A-9; "Trucking: Deregulation Would Have Minor Impact on Service to Small Communities, CBO Says," *BNA DER,* February 29, 1980, p. A-17; Stephen M. Aug, "Eased Truck Rules Won't Hurt Small Towns, Study Says," *Washington Star,* April 11, 1980, p. D-9.

[34] Senate Report 96-641; "Trucking: Administration Supporting Sen. Cannon's Deregulation Bill," p. A-11; "Trucking: DOT Supports ICC Proposal to Allow Truckers to Make Intermediate Stops," *BNA DER,* January 15, 1980, p. A-7; Shifrin, "The Byzantine World of Trucking Industry," p. G-3.

[35] *1980 House Hearings on Trucking Deregulation,* statement of Frank S. Swain of the National Federation of Independent Business, February 21, 1980.

[36] *1980 Senate Hearings on Trucking Deregulation,* statement of the American Trucking Associations, February 27, 1980.

[37] Ibid.

[38] Ibid.

[39] National Meat Association, *Position Paper,* undated.

[40] *1979 Senate Hearings on Trucking Deregulation,* statement of Bernard Imming for the United Fresh Fruit Produce Association, October 30, 1979.

[41] Association of American Railroads, *Position Paper in Opposition to Stevenson Amendment to S. 2245,* undated.

[42] *Congressional Record,* vol. 126 (April 15, 1980), p. S 3601, statement of Senator Hollings (D-S.C.); Senate Report 96-641, pp. 86, 97-98, 101-104.

[43] Ibid., pp. 86, 101-104; *Congressional Record,* vol. 126 (April 15, 1980), pp. S 3601, S 3603.

[44] Senate Report 96-641, pp. 87, 104-106; *Congressional Record,* vol. 126 (April 15, 1980), pp. S 3634-S 3636.

[45] Senate Report 96-641, pp. 106-107.

[46] Remarks of Charles Fields, assistant director, American Farm Bureau, before the Transportation Consumer Action Project Symposium, May 17, 1979.

[47] *1980 House Hearings on Trucking Deregulation,* statement of National Council of Farmer Cooperatives, February 28, 1980.

[48] Senate Report 96-641, pp. 7-9; *Congressional Record,* vol. 126 (April 15, 1980), pp. S 3634-S 3635, statement of Senator Stevenson (D-Ill.); ibid., p. S 3619, statement of Senator Cannon.

[49] Shifrin, "The Byzantine World of Trucking Industry," p. G-3.

[50] Senate Report 96-641, pp. 11-12, 55-56.

[51] *1980 Senate Hearings on Trucking Deregulation,* statement of the American Trucking Associations, February 27, 1980.

[52] See 49 U.S.C. 10761, 11902-11903.

[53] Ibid., statement of Frank S. Swain, National Federation of Independent Business, February 21, 1980.

[54] Shifrin, "Deregulation on Its Way for Interstate Truckers," p. G-3.

[55] Senate Report 96-641, pp. 80-81.

[56] *1979 Senate Hearings on Trucking Deregulation,* statement of Shenefield, December 3, 1979.

[57] Merrill Brown, "Truck Bill Backed," *Washington Post,* February 27, 1980, p. D-6; Carole Shifrin, "High Stakes in Trucking Deregulation," *Washington Post,* March 5, 1980, pp. D-7, D-10; Senate Report 96-641, pp. 13-14; cf. "Railroads: ICC May Propose Limits on Antitrust Immunity," *BNA DER,* April 8, 1980, p. A-4; "Trucking: Administration Supports Sen. Cannon's Deregulation Bill," p. A-11. Single-line rates refer to rates applicable to carriage that does not involve the service of a second carrier. The terms of the Reed-Bulwinkle Act are brought forward at 49 U.S.C. 10706(b).

[58] *1980 Senate Hearings on Trucking Deregulation,* statement of Shenefield, February 26, 1980.

[59] *1979 Senate Hearings on Trucking Deregulation,* statement of Donald F. Kuster for the National Industrial Traffic League, November 17, 1979.

[60] *1979 Joint Senate-House Hearings on Trucking Deregulation,* statement of Richard Warren for the National Association of Manufacturers, November 17, 1979.

[61] Ibid., pp. 88-91, 112-114, minority views of Senators Hollings and Inouye; "Trucking Deregulation Rolling," p. 102; "Trucking: Industry Efforts to Weaken Deregulation Bill Fail in Senate Committee," p. A-12.

[62] Senate Report 96-641, pp. 109-112, minority views of Senators Hollings and Inouye; *Congressional Record,* vol. 126 (April 15, 1980), p. S 3601, statement of Senator Hollings.

[63] *1980 Senate Hearings on Trucking Deregulation,* statement of the American Trucking Associations, February 27, 1980.